The Symbols and Legends of Masonry

By C. H. Vail

ISBN: 978-1-63118-504-5

Foundations of Freemasonry Series

Other Books in this Series and Related Titles

Masonic and Rosicrucian History by M P Hall & H Voorhis (978-1-63118-486-4)

The Kabbalah of Masonry & Related Writings by E Levi &c (978-1-63118-453-6)

Some Deeper Aspects of Masonic Symbolism by A E Waite (978-1-63118-461-1)

Masonic Symbolism of King Solomon's Temple by A Mackey &c (978-1-63118-442-0)

The Old Past Master by Carl H Claudy (978-1-63118-464-2)

Brothers & Builders by Joseph Fort Newton (978-1-63118-506-9)

The Influence of Pythagoras on Freemasonry and Other Essays (978-1-63118-404-8)

Rosicrucians and Speculative Masonry in the Seventeenth Century (978-1-63118-489-5)

The Two Great Pillars of Boaz and Jachin by A Mackey &c (978-1-63118-433-8)

The Regius Poem or Halliwell Manuscript by King Solomon (978-1-63118-447-5)

The Lost Keys of Freemasonry or The Secret of Hiram Abiff (978-1-63118-427-7)

The Master Mason's Handbook by J S M Ward (978-1-63118-474-1)

Masonic Symbolism of the Apron & the Altar by various (978-1-63118-428-4)

Symbolism and Discourses on the Entered Apprentice, Fellowcraft and Master Mason Blue Lodge Degrees by various (978-1-63118-413-0)

Freemasonry in the Medieval or Middle Ages by various (978-1-63118-450-5)

Freemasonry & Catholicism by Max Heindel (978-1-63118-508-3)

Freemasonry, Mithraism and the Ancient Mysteries by various (978-1-63118-407-9)

The Ceremony of Initiation: Analysis & Commentary (978-1-63118-473-4)

Masonic Life of George Washington by Albert G Mackey (978-1-63118-457-4)

The Janeites, The Man Who Would Be King and Other Stories of Freemasonry by Rudyard Kipling (978-1-63118-480-2)

Audio Versions are also Available from Apple, Amazon & Audible

Table of Contents

Introduction…7

Preface…9

The Lodge…13

The Furnishing of the Lodge…16

The Ornaments…18

The All-Seeing Eye…19

The Letter G…20

The Clasped Hands…21

The Triangle and Double Triangle…22

The Light…23

Jacob's Ladder…24

The Right Angled Triangle, or the 47th Problem of Euclid…26

The Lamb-Skin or White Leather Apron…28

Sacred or Ineffable Name…31

The Rite of Circumambulation...35

The Legend of the Winding Stairs...36

The Hiramic Legend and the Master's Degree...39

The Sprig of Acacia...43

The Rite of Discalceation...44

The Stone of Foundation...45

The Lost Word...48

Conclusion...50

INTRODUCTION

From the beginning of Modern Freemasonry's birthdate of 1717, the intelligentsia of humanity have found refuge for safe reflection within the walls of the fraternity. Masonic writers have produced a nearly incalculable amount of written musings on a multitude of esoteric and philosophical subjects, as they relate to the ancient mysteries that Freemasonry currently storehouses. Sadly, most of it appears to have sat largely unread, as American Freemasonry in particular, continues to transform itself into something that bears little resemblance to what it was originally designed to be. The true essence of Freemasonry is not that of blind patriotism or a single-minded national religion but one of Universal Brotherhood and altruism, designed for the betterment not just of its members but of society as a whole. In particular, for those who are not members of the fraternity, as Freemasonry has always acted as a beacon, to help guide humanity through darker times, with the hopes that one day we will collectively reach a truly enlightened age.

It's not uncommon for new members joining the fraternity to find little education within the walls of many modern lodges, in spite of so much written material available to the membership. Many older members are not simply uneducated with regards to real Masonic history and symbology, not to mention the vast arena of related subjects, but they are disinterested in all of it, as well.

Lamp of Trismegistus is doing its part to help preserve humanity's Masonic history by making some of these classics available to those students who are seeking to unearth the knowledge of these ancient colossi. As such, Lamp of Trismegistus offers its readers highlights of Masonic study, culled from a variety of authors and viewpoints, with the hope bringing education back into the fraternity. So, be sure to check out other titles in our *Foundations of Freemasonry Series* as well as our *Theosophical Classics*, *Occult Fiction*, *Paranormal Research Series*, *Esoteric Classics*, *Supernatural Fiction*, *Studies in Buddhism* and our *Christian Apocrypha Series* as well as numerous other subjects; and, don't be afraid to let a little altruism into your own heart or even into your Lodge. You can also download the audio versions of many of these titles from Audible, Amazon or Apple, for learning on the go.

PREFACE

The real secrets of Masonry lie concealed in its symbols and legends.

These symbols and legends are the means by which the divine truths of Masonry are conveyed to the neophyte. This was the method of instruction in the Ancient Mysteries, and it was naturally adopted in the institution of Freemasonry. "To form symbols and to interpret them," says Creuzer, "were the main occupations of the ancient priesthood," and the myths were invented to illustrate a philosophic or religious truth.

Dr. Mackey, after discussing the question of myths, says, "It must be evident, from all that has been said respecting the analogy in origin and design between the Masonic and the ancient religious myths, that no one acquainted with the true science of this subject can, for a moment, contend that all the legends and traditions of the order are, to the very letter, historical facts." (*Symbolism of Freemasonry*, Mackey, p. 207.) He gives as an illustration of this the myth of the Winding Stairs, which, he says, "taken in its literal sense, is, in all its parts, opposed to history and probability."

Again, he calls attention to the myth which traces the origin of Freemasonry to the beginning of the world, "A myth, which is," he says, "even to this day, ignorantly interpreted, by some, as an historical fact, and the reference to which is still preserved in the date of 'anno lucis,' which is affixed to all masonic documents." This he calls a "philosophical myth, symbolizing the idea which analogically connects the creation of physical light in the universe with the birth of masonic or spiritual and intellectual light in the candidate. The one is the type of the other." (Ibid, p. 211.) In the legends of the Master's Degree and of the Royal Arch he points out that there is a commingling of the historical myth and the mythical history so that much care must be taken in discriminating between the different elements.

Dr. Mackey then sums up the duty of a Mason as follows, "He who desires properly to appreciate the profound wisdom of the institution of which he is the disciple, must not be content, with uninquiring credulity, to accept all the traditions that are imparted to him as veritable histories; nor yet, with unphilosophic incredulity, to reject them in a mass, as fabulous inventions. In these extremes there is equal error. 'The myth,' says Hermann, 'is the representation of an idea.' It is for that idea that the student must search in the myths of Masonry. Beneath every one of them there is something richer and more spiritual than the mere narrative. . . Every one, therefore, who desires to be a skillful Mason, must not suppose that the task is accomplished by a perfect knowledge of the mere phraseology of the ritual, by a readiness in opening and closing a lodge, nor by an off-hand capacity to confer degrees. All these are good in their places, but without the internal meaning they are but mere child's play. He must study the myths, the traditions, and the symbols of the order, and learn their true interpretation; for this alone constitutes the science and the philosophy—the end, aim, and design of Speculative Masonry." (Ibid, p. 212, 214.)

These deeper things, as Dr. Mackey intimates, are not found in the monitorial explanations. J. D. Buck, a 32nd degree Mason, in his wonderful book on Mystic Masonry, says, "The most profound secrets of Masonry are not revealed in the Lodge at all. They belong only to the few. . . But these secrets must be sought by the individual himself, and the candidate is debarred from possessing them solely by his own inattention to the hints everywhere given in the ritual of the Lodge, or by his indifference to the subject. If he prefers to treat the whole subject with contempt, and to deny that any such real knowedge exists, it becomes evident that he not only closes the door against the possibility of himself possessing such knowledge, but he also becomes impervious to any evidence of its existence that might come to him at any time. He has no one but himself to blame if he is left in darkness." (*Mystic Masonry*, Buck, p. XXXVI.)

The ritual and monitorial lessons of the Lodge teach nothing new, and the explanations of the symbols are often puerile and inadequate. Albert Pike says, "There is no sight under the sun more pitiful and ludicrous at once, than the spectacle of the Prestons and the Webbs, not to mention the later incarnations of Dullness and Commonplace, undertaking to 'explain' the old symbols of Masonry, and adding to and 'improving' them, or inventing new ones. To the Circle enclosing the central point, and itself traced between two parallel lines, a figure purely Kabbalistic; these persons have added the superimposed Bible, and even reared on that the ladder with three or nine rounds and then given a vapid interpretation of the whole, so profoundly absurd as actually to excite admiration." (*Morals and Dogma*, Pike, P. 105.)

The exegesis is also often crude. This is not strange, as the ritual was written before the days of modern Biblical scholarship, and perhaps it would be well if the ritual were revised. These immature conceptions could be eliminated without affecting the meaning and beauty of the ceremonies. However, if we bear in mind that Masonry does not endorse its legends as literal facts, no harm can be done.

We will now consider some of the symbols and myths of the Fraternity.

THE LODGE

The Lodge represents King Solomon's Temple. The temple is a symbolic image of the universe, and as such is symbolic in all its parts and arrangements, therefore, the temple of Solomon resembles all the temples of antiquity that practiced the Mysteries.

The Hebrews, like other peoples, made much of the system of numbers to convey their hidden meaning. The Holy of Holies formed a cube, corresponding to the number four, which represented manifested nature, while the three sides or faces of the figure, when drawn on a plane surface, represented the Deity, the three aspects of Will, Wisdom and Activity (Intelligence). Everything within the temple was symbolically arranged. The ceiling, supported by twelve columns, represented the twelve months of the year; the borders around the columns and the candlestick with the twelve lights represented the twelve signs of the zodiac; the seven lights, the seven planets; the veils of four colors represented the four elements, etc. In the Royal Arch Degree of the American Rite, the Tabernacle has four veils of different colors, to each of which belongs a banner and on each banner is inscribed one of the four images; the Bull, the Lion, the Man, the Eagle. These constellations answered to the equatorial and solstitial points of 2500 years B.C. The four signs Taurus, Leo, Scorpio, and Aquarius, were termed the fixed signs, and are assigned to the four veils. The Sun entered Taurus at the vernal equinox, Leo at the Summer solstice, Scorpio at the autumnal equinox (for which, on account of its malignant influence, Aquila, the eagle was substituted), and Aquarius at the winter solstice.

Every temple was a representation of the universe, and in them the great lights of Nature played an important part. The images of the Sun, Moon, and Mercury were represented, and even in our Lodge rooms they constitute the three lights, except that for Mercury the Master of the Lodge has been substituted. Eusebius tells us that the officers of the Eleusinian Mysteries were the Hierophant, representing the Great Architect of the Universe; the torch-bearer, representing the Sun; the altar-bearer, representing the Moon; and the sacred herald, representing Mercury. The latter was charged with excluding the profane from the Mysteries.

Every Lodge, as we have said, represents the Temple. The two great columns between which you pass as you enter the Lodge represent the two great pillars, 30 feet 8 inches high; 6 feet 10 inches in diameter, which stood in the porch of the temple on either side of the Eastern gateway. These columns represent the two pillars of Hercules,—the solstices, Capricorn and Cancer, the two gates of heaven,—and were imitations by the Tyrian artist of the columns at the entrance of the temple of Malkarth[1] in Tyre.

---

[1] Also spelt Melqart. The name means "king of the city", and Melqart was the supreme god of Tyre. Reflecting his dual role as both protector of the world and ruler of the underworld, he was often shown holding an Egyptian ankh or lotus flower as a symbol of life and an axe as a symbol of death.

The Lodge is said to be due east and west as King Solomon's Temple was so situated. All the temples of Antiquity were usually thus built. Pythagoras also arranged his assemblies due east and west because he held that motion began in the east and proceeded west. The Egyptian and Mexican Pyramids were also built to the four cardinal points of the compass, while beneath the Temple, extending east and west, was a subterranean cavern used for Initiation. No well-equipped Lodge is lacking in this particular.

THE FURNISHING OF THE LODGE

The Holy Bible, Square and Compasses, together with a Charter or Dispensation, constitute the furnishings of the Lodge.

(1) The Holy Bible. This, in a Christian Lodge, consists of the Old and New Testaments; a Hebrew Lodge would use the Old Testament only; a Muslim Lodge, the Koran; in like manner a Buddhist Lodge could use the Tripitaka, a Hindu Lodge the Vedas, etc. The obligation of the candidate is always taken on the Sacred Book of his religion, for his Holy Bible is his Light, in accordance with which he should live and walk.

(2) The Square and Compasses. These symbols are perhaps the most familiar to the general public of any in Masonry. I need not dwell on the lessons in morality which the square and compasses teach. Masonry is, however, something more than a system of morality, and it is this inner significance that I have endeavored to set forth.

There is a science and philosophy concealed in these symbols which Dr. Buck explains as follows: "The Square with its one right angle and its scale of measurements applies to surfaces and solids, and deals with the apparently fixed states of matter. It represents solidarity, symmetry and proportion; and this involves the sciences of arithmetic and geometry. The Compasses with moveable angle set in the Lodge at an angle of 60 degrees, applies to the circle and the sphere; to movements and revolutions. In a general sense, the square is a symbol of matter and the earth; the Compasses of Spirit and the heavens." (*Mystic Masonry*, Buck, P. 242.)

The position of the Square and Compasses indicates the progress of the candidate from Entered Apprentice to that of Master Mason.

THE ORNAMENTS

The Ornaments of a Lodge are the Mosaic Pavement, the Indented Tessel, and the Blazing Star.

The Mosaic Pavement is supposed to represent the ground floor of King Solomon's Temple; the Indented Tessel, the border or skirting surrounding it. There is no evidence that either existed in the ancient temple, but the symbol is significant as it denotes the checkered course of life, also the two opposing principles in Nature,—Light and Darkness, Michael and Satan, Balder and Loki, Ormuzd[2] and Ahriman, etc.

The Blazing Star also represents these two principles. If the point is turned upward it represents God, Good, Order, or the Lamb of Ormuzd and St. John; if the point is turned downward it denotes Lucifer, Evil, Disorder, or the accursed Goat of Mendes and the Mysteries. The Blazing Star or Pentagram also represents the human body,—the five points representing the four limbs and head. It is thus called the sign of the Microcosm. All the Mysteries of Magic were said to be summed up in this symbol. Paracelsus pronounces it the greatest and most potent of all signs.

---

[2] Ahura Mazda

THE ALL-SEEING EYE

This symbol, in the Ancient Mysteries, indicated the sight that annuls time and space. This is the symbol of the higher clairvoyance. The Master always possessed this sight. In India this All Seeing Eye was called the Eye of Siva. The Egyptians represented Osiris by the symbol of an open eye, and placed this hieroglyphic of him in all their temples. In the Lodge the All Seeing Eye represents the Omniscence of God, —The Eye that never sleeps. It may also represent, as in the Ancient Mysteries, the higher vision.

THE LETTER G

This letter is the natural symbol among English speaking people for God. It is a substitute in American Lodges for the Hebrew Yod, which is the Kabbalistic symbol for unity. In France the letter Yod is put in the Blazing Star.

THE CLASPED HANDS

This symbol was used by Pythagoras and represented the sacred number ten—the number expressed by the mysterious Tetractys. This figure was represented in the form of the triangle. The Hebrews formed it with the letters of the Divine Name. Both Pythagoras and the Hebrew priests borrowed the figure from the sacred science of Egypt.

THE TRIANGLE AND DOUBLE TRIANGLE

All the nations of antiquity considered the triangle as sacred. It was one of the most common symbols for the Deity. The three sides typify the three aspects of God—Will, Wisdom and Intelligence. Here we have the Trinity in Unity.

The double triangle interlaced, symbolizes the manifested universe—the union of spirit and matter. The triangle pointing upward is spirit or fire ; the one pointing downward is matter or water. One represents the descent of spirit into matter, the other the ascent of matter to spirit. The union of the two, in the manifested universe, is inseparable. This double triangle is used in India to symbolize two Hindu Gods, or rather the two aspects of Ishvara—Siva and Vishnu. It also represents the six points, the senary, which with the point in the center is the septinary.

THE LIGHT

There are three greater and three lesser lights in Masonry, and though the ritual does not give any explanation of these symbols, there is an important meaning connected with them. The Sun is an ancient symbol of the Logos—it signifies the male aspect, the life-giving and generative power. God is the source of light, and light is the cause of life. The Moon represents the passive, or female aspect of Nature.

JACOB'S LADDER

The mystical ladder which Jacob in his vision saw, extending from earth to heaven, was a common symbol in the Ancient Mysteries, and was always composed of seven steps or rounds. The ladder symbolized the progress of man from his present to higher conditions—each round representing one of the seven stages of his evolutionary progress. In the Mysteries of Persia and India this mystic ladder was an important symbol, especially in the former, where a ladder of seven rounds was erected in each of their temples.

The seven steps also correspond to the seven gates through which the candidate was passed successively in his journeyings through the seven caverns of Initiation, and symbolized the seven conditions or subplanes of Hades. The seven steps, seven gates, seven halls, seven worlds, seven planes, etc., are all symbols of the various stages of the soul's progress.

The ancient Initiates held that the evolution of the human soul took place through a series of seven globes situated on the three lower planes of the universe. The life wave passes seven times round this world-chain, and through seven stages on each globe. The progress involves a downward and an upward arc— a descent of spirit into matter and a re-ascent of spirit to God. This is symbolized in Jacob's vision by the angels ascending and descending.

Jacob's ladder is sometimes misrepresented with three or nine rounds; it should have seven. Dr. Mackey says that "The error arose from the ignorance of those inventors who first engraved the masonic symbols for our monitors. The ladder of Masonry, like the equipollent ladders of its kindred institutions, always had seven steps, although in modem times the three principal or upper ones are alone alluded to. These rounds, beginning at the lowest, are Temperance, Fortitude, Prudence, Justice, Faith, Hope, and Charity." (*The Symbolism of Freemasonry*, Mackey, p. 120.) The application of these virtues, however, is a later addition to symbolism.

The seven rounds are also emblematical of the seven planes of the universe—physical, astral, mental buddhic, atmic, anupadika and adi; the seven ancient elements—earth, water, fire, air, ether, and two unnamed; the seven subplanes of the astral world— astral solid, liquid, gaseous, etheric, super-etheric, subatomic, and atomic; the seven metals—lead, quicksilver, copper, tin, iron, silver, and gold; the seven colors—black, purple, green, blue, red, white, and yellow; the seven stones—diamond, amethyst, emerald, sapphire, ruby, pearl, and topaz; the seven ancient planets—Saturn, Mercury, Venus, Jupiter, Mars, Luna and Sol. Thus the seven-stepped ladder had various applications and correspondences. Its presence in the Masonic institutions is evidence of the close analogy between Freemasonry and the Ancient Mysteries.

THE RIGHT ANGLED TRIANGLE, OR THE 47TH PROBLEM OF EUCLID

This is one of the most important symbols of antiquity. The perpendicular line, whose measurement is 3, represents the active, male principle; the base line, whose measurement is 4, represents the passive, female principle; and their union, or the addition of the squares of these numbers, will produce a square whose root will be the hypotheneuse,—a line measured by 5 and representing the universe. The square of the perpendicular and base, 9+16=25, the square root of which is 5, the number of the hypotheneuse. It was taught in all the Mysteries that the union of the male and female principles of Nature produced the universe. This is the occult meaning of the 47th problem of Euclid—the sum of the squares of the perpendicular and base of a right angle triangle equals the square of the hypotheneuse. This is a symbol of perfect proportion between number and forms; between spirit and matter.

The three sides of the triangle bear the proportions, as we have seen, of 3, 4, and 5, and 32+42=52, or 9+16=25; also 9+16+25=50. Thus the number 50 is based on the proportion of the sides of the right angled triangle.

Philo speaks of two series, which he calls triangles and squares; namely, 1, 3, 6, 10 and 1, 4, 9, 16. With regard to the triangle series 1, 3, 6, 10, it is interesting to note that 1=1; 3=1+2; 6=1+2+3; and 10=1+2+3+4. In the square series, 1, 4, 9, 16; 1=1^2; 4=2^2; 9=3^2; and 16=4^2; 1+3+6+10=20;

and 1+4+9+16=30; and 20+30=50; 50 was a sacred number, and was derived from the right angled triangle. The greatest Jewish festival (Jubilee) took place every fifty years.

THE LAMB-SKIN OR WHITE LEATHER APRON

In the Ancient Mysteries the investiture of the Apron formed an essential part of the ceremony of Initiation. The Apron and White Robe were symbols of purity. In Persia the investiture was exceedingly imposing. The candidate having taken the oath of secrecy, was given the insignia of the Order—the Girdle, the Tiara, the White Apron and the Purple Tunic. The Japanese candidate was also clothed in certain Garments which consisted of a Loose Tunic and White Apron bound round the loins with a girdle. In the degree of holiness practiced by the Pharisees the "noviciate" was also given an Apron as a symbol of purity. The Essenes and Druids invested their candidates with a White Robe, and the Scandinavians gave the candidate a White Shield. In all these ceremonies whatever the material or form, the symbolic significance was always the same. The White Apron of Masonry was derived from these ancient ceremonies, and is one of the most significant symbols in our Order; the color "White" having been an emblem of Light and Purity from time immemorial.

The shape and combination of the Masonic Apron is that of a triangle overlapping a square, representing the occult septenary nature of man. The triangle symbolize? spirit, or the three highest principles; the square or quaternary the four lowest. Each principle is correlated to a plane, a round and a race. The spiritual triad is the spiritual body of St. Paul, and the quaternary the natural body. The triad, which is the immortal part of man, contains potentially all the powers of Divinity; and to develop these latent attributes it must descend into matter—the triangle must incarnate in the square. This is represented in Masonry by the degree of Entered Apprentice, and is symbolized by the way in which the Apprentice is taught to wear his Apron. The spiritual is subordinate to the material—earthly desires and passions rule supreme. But the candidate is here to learn to subdue his passions; his partial success is represented by the degree of Fellow Craft, and is symbolized by the way he wears his Apron in that degree. The complete triumph of the spiritual is represented by the Master Mason degree, and is' again indicated by the Apron. This state was represented in the Ancient Mysteries by the mystical death and resurrection of the candidate. The perfected Initiate has mastered his lower nature and has become the Perfect Man,—Hermes, Buddha, or Christ.

The symbolism of the Apron is indeed far reaching.

Let every Mason remember how he impersonated the Grand Master. He should never forget its deep significance. In the Ancient Mysteries the candidate did not merely impersonate' the Master, he himself became the Master—the ceremony merely symbolizing what he became. It is a mistake to suppose, as some writers have, that the candidate in the mystic rites was merely representing the events connected with the tragedy of the Master or God from whom the Mysteries derived their name. The story of the Master or God was wholly an allegory of the experiences of the Initiate, while the rites were hut typical of the various stages in the growth of the soul.

In the process of becoming a Christ he represents all those who have attained the Christ state, for all masters have passed through the experience symbolized by the Myth.

Masonry has a truer conception than any exoteric religion, for these religions take the symbol for the thing symbolized, but Masonry, in making the candidate impersonate Hiram, has preserved the original teaching. Hiram is identical with the Sun-Gods of all nations—it is a universal glyph, for all real Initiation is an internal process, a regeneration, the consummation of which is the Perfect Man or Master, the goal of human evolution.

In the Ancient Mysteries there was a further Rite which symbolized the next stage, that of union with the Divine, the At-One-Ment. This was the Ascension, and is symbolized by the square enclosed in the triangle. The lower nature is here refined and "ascends to the Father." God is All in All.

As we have already said, each principle in man's constitution is correlated to a plane. A knowledge of these planes would enable a man by a trained will to direct the forces on each plane. Such is the power of a real Master.

SACRED OR INEFFABLE NAME

This symbol was universal in ancient times, for every nation of antiquity had its Sacred Name or Ineffable Word. The Hebrew symbol consists of four letters, Yod, He, Vau, He, and is called the Tetragrammaton, or four lettered word. This word was said to have been communicated by God to Moses at the burning bush. The name was held most sacred by the Jews, but its meaning and proper pronunciation has long been obscured.

Before the invention of the masoretic points the pronunciation of a word in the Hebrew language could not be known by the characters themselves, so it was easy in the course of time to lose the proper pronunciation. Especially so, as at the beginning of the Hellenistic age the use of the name was reserved for the temple. At the beginning of the Christian era, Philo writes, "The four letters may be mentioned or heard only by holy men whose ears and tongues are prepared by wisdom,, and by no others in any place whatsoever." In the course of time the pronunciation of the name, even by the temple priests, fell into disuse, and the manner of its pronunciation at length became a secret entrusted only to the few. While the word was being withdrawn from common use, it was pronounced "Adonai" in the scripture, and when the vowel points were introduced those that belonged to Adonai were placed under the Tetragrammaton.

The word itself is a symbol; the letters are probably arranged as a blind. As they stand in the Tetragrammaton they have no significance. They do not represent any real Hebrew word. Now if we apply the Hebrew method of halving or transposing letters which was used to conceal the meaning of a word, or rather if we reverse the process which may have been employed, we get instead of Y. H. V. H., H. V. H. Y. Before the introduction of vowel signs, certain weak consonants such as Yod and Vau, were sometimes used to indicate vowel sounds, so we frequently see I or E given as an equivalent for Yod, and U or O given for Vau. Even Yod is sometimes given as Jod, and Vau as Waw, so we have the name given as Y. H. V. H. or I. H. V. H. or J. H. V. H., or Y. H, W. H., or I. H. O. H., etc.

Now the personal pronouns He and She are written in Hebrew with the signs He, Vau, A-leph, and He, Yod, Aleph. When Aleph terminates a word, and has no vowel immediately preceding or following, if is usually dropped. Now if we drop the final Aleph we have the transposed Tetragrammaton, H. V. H. Y., which are the personal pronouns He and She, the male and female, representing the two great principles of nature,—the dual aspect of the Second Logos.

Now if we turn to the Kabbalah, which contains some portions of the secret teachings of the Jews, we shall find that this great principle is the exact meaning of the Tetragrammaton. It does not represent the Absolute Deity, or the Unmanifested Logos, but it does represent the manifested, the first emanation—Adam Kadmon. The two aspects of Being which are potential in the First Logo, become manifested in the later stages of evolution. This name represents the four worlds—Alseluth, signified by Yod, Briah by He, Yezerah by Vau, and Asiah by the Second He. The source of the Tetragrammaton is Absolute Deity, Ain-Soph, the Causeless Cause. The Tetragrammaton is also the Sephiroth, which are ten in number, and emanate one from the other. The highest is Kether, the Crown; then comes Chockmah and Binah, the male and female principles. From these emanate the other seven. The very fact that the meaning of the Tetragrammaton is identical with the words obtained by transposing the letters, is sufficient evidence that the word was really H. V. (or W. U. O.) H. Y. (or J. I. E.), according to the equivalents adopted for the signs—whether interpreted as consonants or vowels—and the names given to the signs.

The meaning and pronunciation of the word was carefully guarded. There is no hint given in the ritual for this secrecy, but there is a scientific reason, for the mystic Word has to do with the science of rhythmic vibrations which is the key to the equilibrium of all forces. In all mysticism the knowledge of names meant the possession of powers. The spoken name gave one the power of the name. It is interesting to note how the Jews worked this idea into their system. In the Talmud the wonderful works of Jesus are ascribed to his use of the Sacred Name. According to early traditions the knowledge whereby he wrought these works was learned in Egypt, but in the developed Toldoth the "word of power" was the Holy Name,—the Tetgrammaton.

All nations of antiquity had their Sacred Names, which were "Words of Power." These names were formed by taking a letter which conveyed a meaning and adding other letters each having a meaning; the whole word thus formed constituting a Sacred Name or Word, which contains some great truth. These Names were Words of Power, for, as the unfolding consciousness realizes one truth after another and becomes that truth, it rules. In Persia the Sacred Name was H. O. M., in India A. U. M., in Scandinavia I. O. W., in Greece I. A. O., etc.

THE RITE OF CIRCUMAMBULATION

This Rite again connects Freemasonry with the Ancient Mysteries. It consists in a formal procession around the altar, and originally alluded to the apparent course of the sun which is from east to west. In ancient Greece the priests, during the Rites of sacrifice, walked three times around the altar while chanting a sacred hymn, which was divided into three parts, and each part was to be sung at a particular point in the procession.

The analogy between this practice of the ancients and the recitations of a passage of Scripture in the Masonic circumambulation' is quite apparent. In making this circuit it was considered necessary that the right side should always be next to the altar, and so the procession moved from west to the north, then east, south, west and then to the north again. We find the same Rite among the Romans, Druids, and Hindus. In all these ceremonies they were "imitating the example of the sun and following his beneficent course."

THE LEGEND OF THE WINDING STAIRS

This Legend is connected with the Fellow Craft degree. It is based upon I Kings, vi, 8, "The door for the middle chamber was in the right side of the house; and they went up with winding stairs into the middle chamber, and out of the middle into the third."

"Out of this slender material," says Dr. Mackey, "has been constructed an allegory, which, if properly considered in its symbolical relations, will be found to be of surpassing beauty. But it is only as a symbol that we can regard this whole tradition; for the historical facts and the architectural details alike forbid us for a moment to suppose that the legend, as it is rehearsed in the second degree of Masonry, is anything more than a magnificent philosophical myth." (*The Symbolism of Freemasonry*, Mackey, p. 215.)

The lesson which this legend teaches is not difficult to discover. Freemasonry is a speculative science which has for its object the investigation of divine truth. The candidate is in search of more light, and as all the ceremonies denote a progress from a lower to a higher state, he is always progressing. This fundamental symbolism of Masonry is found in each degree. There is the mystical ladder, the ceremony of circumambulation, the restoration to life, etc. The Legend of the Winding Stairs symbolizes the same fact—the ascent of man from ignorance to knowledge, from darkness to light, from death to life.

The steps of the Winding Stairs commenced on the porch of the Temple. This indicates the beginning of the masonic life—the preparation for entering the temple.

It is curious to note that the number of steps in all the systems has been odd. This probably is due to the fact that the symbolism of numbers was borrowed from Pythagoras, in whose system of philosophy the odd numbers were regarded as sacred, though the number of steps has greatly varied. Tracing boards have been found in which only five steps are represented, and others which denote seven. At one time in England the number was thirty-eight, which was reduced to thirty-seven, and in this country the number has been reduced to fifteen. Perhaps five would be the more appropriate as the stairs only extended to the middle chamber. The number seven, corresponding to the number of rounds in the mystic ladder, would indicate the attainment of perfection— the Holy of Holies. We might say that the complete stairs are composed of seven steps,—three carrying the candidate into the ground floor of the temple, two into the middle, and two into the inner sanctuary. The general symbolism of the Legend is not affected by the number of steps, or the method of division.

The candidate who succeeds in climbing the Winding Stairs will receive his reward. What is the reward or wages of the Speculative Mason? Not silver nor gold, but Truth. Yet the whole of divine truth cannot be imparted to the Fellow Craft. The Middle Chamber, then, where he receives his wages, is symbolical of the Fellow Craft degree, and the wages are appropriate to the degree of his progress.

To again quote Dr. Mackey, "It is, then, as a symbol, and a symbol only, that we must study this beautiful legend of the Winding Stairs. If we attempt to adopt it as an historical fact, the absurdity of its details stares us in the face, and wise men will wonder at our credulity. Its inventors had no desire thus to impose upon our folly; but offering it to us as a great philosophical myth, they did not for a moment suppose that we would pass over its sublime moral teachings to accept the allegory as an historical narrative, without meaning, and wholly irreconcilable with the records of Scripture, and opposed by all the principles of probability. To suppose that eighty thousand craftsmen were weekly paid in the narrow precincts of the temple chambers, is simply to suppose an absurdity." (Ibid, p. 226.)

We must guard against the materialization of our allegories and symbols. Remember Masonry is a "system of morality, veiled in allegory and illustrated by symbols." To regard the myths as history is to miss the truth which the symbols were designed to teach. No intelligent Mason will fall into this error.

THE HIRAM LEGEND AND THE MASTER'S DEGREE

The Hiram Legend and the Master's Degree are derived from the Mysteries. They are the latest expression of the old Sun Myth and the Ancient Rite.

Dr. Mackey, in speaking of the symbol of Hiram, says, "It was evidently borrowed from the pagan Mysteries, where Bacchus, Adonis, Proserpina, and a host of other apotheosized beings play the same role that Hiram does in the Masonic Mysteries." (Ibid, p. 20.)

I have given various forms of these Legends—the Osiris, Atys, Hu, Balder, and others. In each of them the Hero of the Myth dies or is deprived of life, is laid away in the tomb, and rises again from the grave. This ceremony was called the mystical death and resurrection.

The legend represents the activity of the Logos in the cosmos, and the mystic life of the Initiate. The ancient legends and symbols always have a double meaning and sometimes more. The lectures on True Initiation set forth in detail the two aspects of the Sun Myth—the mythic and the mystic. To the uninitiated the cosmic or mythic aspect of the legend was the only one seen, thus the Rites were supposed by them merely to typify the death and resurrection of some Hero or Demi God, as Osiris, Mithra, Atys, A'donis, Tammuz, etc., and so the Sun was worshipped under these titles. Perhaps this was natural enough, for the visible Sun was a symbol not only of the Logos, the Spiritual Sun, but also of the Initiate. The yearly course of the Sun represented in one aspect the mystic life of the Initiate.

You will recall that in the Hindu Mysteries when the candidate reached the south in his circuits, he said, "I copy the example of the Sun, and follow his beneficent course." This example was not merely external. The Sun is a symbol of the Logos, and its yearly course typifies the work of the Logos, so that the candidate, by representing the Sun and following his course, is really following the example of the Logos;—the Sun Myth typifying both the activity of the Logos and the mystic life of the Initiate.

In the true Mysteries the Rites symbolized the various stages of this mystic life.

Complete mastery over the lower nature was typified by placing the candidate in a trance and laying him away in a sepulcher for three days and nights. In the Pseudo Mysteries the aspirant was confined in a cell in his normal state, and kept there in fear and darkness that he might reflect on the seriousness of the step taken, and be better prepared to receive the mysterious truths bequeathed from the ancient days. This was the symbolical death, the deliverance from which was called the resurrection. While confined in his cell the search for the Hero was made and his body finally found.

The Master Mason will here see the source of the Hiram Legend, and the Master's Degree. I am not permitted to say more, neither is it necessary for those who are qualified will understand. Mr. Singleton, 33rd degree, after describing the mystical death in the Ancient Mysteries, says, "The Intelligent Mason will, from this, discover the origin of the Rites in the 3rd Degree of Symbolic Masonry and the 5th and 31st Degrees, A. A. S. R. The Mysteries, in all their forms, were funereal. They celebrated the mystical death and revivification of some individual by the use of emblems, symbols, and allegorical representations." (*History of Freemasonry and Concordant Orders*, p. 73.) Mr. Singleton is here in error in regard to the purpose of the Mysteries, if he means that they merely celebrated the mystical death and resurrection of some one individual. The ceremonies of Initiation symbolized the progress of the human soul, and the mystical death and resurrection were experienced by every Initiate. Perhaps in the latter days of the Mysteries, when no true Initiation took place, the ceremonies may have been considered as symbolizing the experiences of some special individual, but such was not the case in the true Mysteries.

We see thus that the story of Hiram is but a variation of the ancient and universal legend, in which Osiris, Adonis, Dionysus, Balder, Hu, and many more have played the principal part. Some call Hiram a "mythical symbol." This is true, but he is also a mystical symbol. Mythically Hiram is the Sun, a symbol of the Logos; mystically he is the perfect Initiate, the Grand Master. The myth was not intended to add to the facts of history, but, as De Witte points out, "to illustrate a philosophical or religious truth."

We must here utter a protest against the sectarian interpretation of the Master Mason's degree. It is true that the degree embraces the inner truths of Christianity, in common with all the mystic teaching. But the origin of the degree and all its symbols and legends were derived from the Ancient Mysteries, and to call the degree a Christian institution, as do Hutchinson and Oliver, is erroneous. Dr. Mackey, in speaking of this tendency to Christianize Masonry, says, "We find Christian Masonic writers indulging in it almost to an unwarrantable excess, and by the extent of their sectarian interpretations materially affecting the cosmopolitan character of the institution. This tendency to Christianization has, in some instances, been so universal, and has prevailed for so long a period, that certain symbols and myths have been, in this way, so deeply and thoroughly imbued with the Christian element as. to leave those who have not penetrated into the cause of this peculiarity, in doubt whether they should attribute to the symbol an ancient or a modern and Christian origin. . . It is in this way that Masonry has, by a sort of inevitable process (when we look to the religious sentiment of the interpreters), been Christianized. . . I do not object to the system when the interpretation is not strained. . . all that I contend for is, that such interpretations are modern, and that they do not belong to, although they may often be deduced from, the ancient system." (*The Symbolism of Freemasonry*, Mackey, pp. 238, 246.)

THE SPRIG OF ACACIA

In all the Ancient Mysteries there were sacred plants which were symbols of Initiation. The myrtle was used in the Mysteries of Greece, the areca in the Egyptian Mysteries, the mistletoe in the Druidical Mysteries, the lotus in the Indian Rites, the lettuce in the Mysteries of Adonis, etc. Masonry has borrowed this custom from the ancient;- and adopted the acacia, which was sacred among the Hebrews, as its mystic symbol.

The acacia was a sacred tree which grew abundantly in the vicinity of Jerusalem, The sanctuary of the tabernacle and the holy ark were constructed from this wood, and the tree ever afterwards was regarded as sacred.

This symbol has several meanings, but for our purpose we need mention only the primary and original meaning which is Initiation, and its use as a symbol of immortality and innocence. These are closely connected and must be considered together to get the full meaning of the symbol. In olden days Initiation was based upon innocence; that is, upon purity of life, and the Initiation brought a realization of immortality.

THE RITE OF DISCALCEATION

This Rite refers to the act of uncovering the feet on approaching holy ground. It is a symbol of reverence, and was a common practice among all the nations of antiquity. The priests always offered sacrifices with uncovered feet. Pythagoras instructed his disciples to offer sacrifices and worship with their shoes off. The Mohammedans, when about to perform their devotions, always leave their slippers at the door of the Mosque. The Druids practiced the same custom whenever they celebrated the sacred rites. The Peruvians also left their shoes on the porch when they entered the temple. Dr. Oliver tells us that "The same usage prevailed equally in India, and the islands to the west of Europe; and even the American savages thought that uncovering the feet, while in the act of devotion, was a sublime method of paying honor to the Deity."

The Jewish lawgivers adopted this sign of reverence, and the symbolism has descended to us. The application of the symbol to the third degree is well known to every Mason.

THE STONE OF FOUNDATION

This is the most important symbol of the Royal Arch degree. It must not be confounded with any of the other stone symbols, such as the corner-stone, the key-stone, or the cape-stone.

In the first place we need to understand that the symbol is purely allegorical. To accept it in a literal sense will present, as Dr. Mackey says, "Absurdities and puerilities which would not occur if the Stone of Foundation was received, as it really is, as a philosophical myth, conveying a most profound and beautiful symbolism. Read in this spirit, as all the legends of Masonry should be read, the mythical story of the Stone of Foundation becomes one of the most important and interesting of all the Masonic symbols."

We have not time to trace the legendary history of the Stone of Foundation—probably more legends are connected with this stone than with any other Masonic symbol. The Masonic legends of the Stone of Foundation, like nearly all that are of Jewish origin, are derived from the Jewish Talmud, and owe their origin to the imaginative genius of the Talmudic writers. But there is this difference between Talmudists and Masons. The former accept all these traditions, with their puerilities, anachronisms, and absurdities, as historical, while the intelligent Mason receives them as allegories.

It would be interesting, did space permit, to give in full these Rabbinical reveries, and also the Masonic, traditions based upon them. But I can only outline the tradition.

The Talmudic legends tell us that Enoch built a subterranean temple on Mount Moriah, consisting of nine vaults situated beneath each other and communicating by apertures left in each vault. In the lowest arch he deposited a cubical stone, called afterwards the Stone of Foundation, on which had been inscribed the ineffable name of God. He then made a door of stone, with a ring in it, and placed it over the opening of the uppermost arch, and covered it so that it could not be seen. In the destruction of the world by the deluge all trace of the subterranean temple was lost, but when David was digging for the foundation of the Temple, he discovered, in the lowest depths of the excavation, a certain stone on which the name of God was inscribed. This stone he removed and deposited in the Holy of Holies. It was a favorite theory of the Talmud legend makers that David laid the foundation upon which Solomon built the temple. The Masonic tradition is substantially the same as the Rabbinical, except that it substitutes Solomon for David as the discoverer of the stone, and makes him deposit it in the crypt of the temple, where it remained until the foundation of the second temple was laid, when it was discovered and placed in the Holy of Holies.

These legends, in the light of historical narratives, would be, as Lee says, "so many idle and absurd conceits," as facts, but as allegories they contain an important symbolism.

The symbolism and worship of stones in ancient times was almost universal. The Greeks originally used unhewn stones of a cubical form to represent their Gods. These consecrated stones were placed before the doors of the houses in Athens, also in front of the temples, in the schools and libraries, and at the corners of the streets.

The Thebans worshiped Bacchus under the form of a square stone: Arnobius says that Cybele was represented by a small stone of black color, and Eusebius cites Porphyry as saying that the ancients represented the Deity by a black stone because his nature was obscure; and inscrutable. The Mohammedans also have a black stone, which was formerly worshiped and is still much reverenced by Musselmen. The Druids represented their Gods by cubical stones, and we also find that the early American races worshiped square stones. These citations are taken from Mackey's "Symbolism of Freemasonry." They might easily be extended, but those given will suffice to show that everywhere in the ancient world cubical stones were used as a symbol of the Deity.

These mystical stones were all symbolic, and the legends connected with them allegories. The Masonic Stone and legend are no exceptions; the Stone of Foundation is but a symbol of the Deity.

THE LOST WORD

The symbol of the Lost Word and the legend of the search for it, embodies the whole design of Freemasonry. The primary object of Freemasonry is the. search after Divine Truth. The Word is a symbol of this Divine Truth, and this truth is the key to the "Science of the Soul." The real Master, then, is one learned in the Divine Science—a "Moses" to lead the neophyte through a wilderness of experience, from his ignorant self to a knowledge of his true Self, a conscious union with God.

The symbolism of the Lost Word may be applied to the degradation of the Ancient Mysteries which resulted in the loss of the real Word—the knowledge of occult science. From that time to this, men have ever been in search of the real Word, and although but few have been able to regain the knowledge of the true Mysteries, others have often caught glimpses of the inner meaning, which is symbolized by the Substituted Word. That the symbolism is not well understood is evident from the fact that but few Masons, if any, to-day possess the knowledge and power implied in the symbols and legends of the Order; for this reason only "The Substitute"—monitorial explanation—"is given to the neophyte until he, perhaps in future generations, shall find the True Word."

That Masonry was in search of the meaning of this symbolic Word, is clearly proven by the insight of the Revisionists in 1717, and the fact that Symbolic Masonry did not pretend to give the candidate the Lost Word. They knew that the Word was no mere name, but a knowledge of occult science which could only be attained by soul development. Real Mastership must again be realized before the Lost Word can be found, and such realization must of necessity be the experience of each individual brother by whom it is found.

The use made of the tradition of the recovery of the Lost Word, and its impartation in the Royal Arch degree, shows that the later degree makers little realized the meaning of the symbolism. They mistook the symbol for the thing symbolized. The Royal Arch degree can only give the symbol. The real Word, which holds the inner meaning and the power of the symbol, is still a mystery. To understand this mystic symbol, and all that it implies, is to possess the key to the science of sciences—the real Knowledge or Word of Power.

CONCLUSION

We will now bring this series of lectures to a close. We have seen that Masonry is modeled on the Ancient Mysteries, and derives its important symbols and legends from that source. Is this a mere coincidence? Was there meant to be only a similarity in outward form? We cannot so believe; the analogy is far too close. The men who formulated the ritual very well knew what they were doing. We believe that the secret vaults contain jewels not yet discovered, and it should be the work of every true Mason to search diligently for "More Light." To discover the full meaning of the glyphs and allegories is to revive the Ancient Wisdom, the Secret Doctrine of Antiquity, the real Lost Word. That such Wisdom once existed will not be denied by any intelligent Mason, for the whole superstructure of the Order is based upon the traditions of its existence. Dr. Buck says, "Instead of being an imitation of the Mysteries of Antiquity, Masonry should become their Restoration and Perpetuation through the coming centuries, not by relaxing its discipline, or changing its ritual, but by deepening the learning, intensifying the zeal and elevating the aim of every Brother throughout the world."

We have seen that the Masters of old were true Occultists—Masters of Divine Science. Masonry has preserved for us the names that indicate the reality of occult knowledge and power in the Perfect and Sublime Master, Prince Adept, Sublime Prince of the Royal Secret, etc. If these names do not imply what I have suggested they are a mere farce and should be abolished. That they are empty titles to-day all will agree; many having recognized this fact, are calling for their abolition. But I hold that instead of abolishing the titles we should endeavor to make them stand, in fact, for what in name they indicate. This would be in line with the ancient tradition—a recovery of the real Lost Word, the key to the Science of Knowledge. Every Mason should labor assiduously for the realization of this ideal. Let us not be content with the mere rudiments of our philosophy. "That skill," says Dr. Mackey, "which consists in repeating with fluency and precision, the ordinary lectures, in complying with all the ceremonial requisitions of the ritual, or the giving, with sufficient accuracy, the appointed modes of recognition, pertains only to the very rudiments of the masonic science." There are many to-day who are not satisfied with these preliminary acquirements, and the cry for "More Light" is being heard in every quarter of the Masonic world. Intelligent Masons are beginning to realize that there is something more in our symbols and legends, and they are seeking their inner and ultimate meaning.

Let us aid in this work by making our Lodges schools, our labor study, our wages learning, thus may we attain that knowledge of Divine Truth which shall truly make us Master Masons.

So mote it be.

www.ingramcontent.com/pod-product-compliance
Lightning Source LLC
LaVergne TN
LVHW050947080826
845145LV00004B/1438

* 9 7 8 1 6 3 1 1 8 5 0 4 5 *